IF YOU'RE HAPPY AND YOU KNOW IT

EIGHTEEN STORY SONGS SET TO PICTURES BY

NICKI WEISS

MUSIC ARRANGED BY JOHN KRUMICH

GREENWILLOW BOOKS, NEW YORK

TABLE OF CONTENTS

Special thanks to John Krumich and Tom Glazer for their help.

Gouache paints and colored pencils were combined for the full-color art. The song titles, lettering, and music notation were all drawn by the illustrator. The music was arranged by John Krumich.

Library of Congress Cataloging-in-Publication Data

If you're happy and you know it.
Melodies with chord symbols.
Summary: An illustrated collection of camp songs and traditional songs with piano and guitar music, including "A Tisket, a Tasket," "Pop! Goes the Weasel," and "Do Your Ears Hang Low?"
1. Children's songs.   2. Folk-songs.
[1. Folk songs. 2. Songs]   I. Weiss, Nicki, ill.
M1992.I42 1987   86-753170
ISBN 0-688-06444-2

FOR MY FATHER and CAROL and SAM

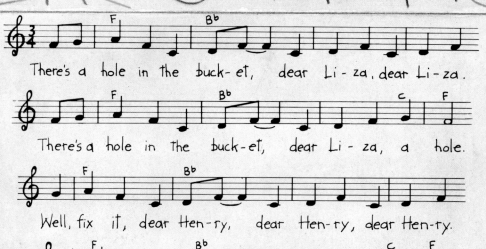

There's a hole in the buck-et, dear Li-za, dear Li-za.

There's a hole in the buck-et, dear Li-za, a hole.

Well, fix it, dear Hen-ry, dear Hen-ry, dear Hen-ry.

Well, fix it, dear Hen-ry, dear Hen-ry, fix it!

2

With what shall I fix it, dear Liza, dear Liza?

With what shall I fix it, dear Liza, with what?

With straw, dear Henry, dear Henry, dear Henry.

With straw, dear Henry, dear Henry, with straw.

3

The straw is too long, dear Liza, dear Liza.

The straw is too long, dear Liza, too long.

Then cut it, dear Henry, dear Henry, dear Henry.

Then cut it, dear Henry, dear Henry, cut it.

4

With what shall I cut it, dear Liza, dear Liza?

With what shall I cut it, dear Liza, with what?

With a knife, dear Henry, dear Henry, dear Henry.

With a knife, dear Henry, dear Henry, a knife.

5

The knife is too dull, dear Liza, dear Liza.

The knife is too dull, dear Liza, too dull.

Then sharpen it, dear Henry, dear Henry, dear Henry.

Then sharpen it, dear Henry, dear Henry, sharpen it.

6

With what shall I sharpen it, dear Liza, dear Liza?

With what shall I sharpen it, dear Liza, with what?

With a stone, dear Henry, dear Henry, dear Henry.

With a stone, dear Henry, dear Henry, a stone.

7

The stone is too dry, dear Liza, dear Liza.

The stone is too dry, dear Liza, too dry.

Then wet it, dear Henry, dear Henry, dear Henry.

Then wet it, dear Henry, dear Henry, wet it.

8

With what shall I wet it, dear Liza, dear Liza?

With what shall I wet it, dear Liza, with what?

With water, dear Henry, dear Henry, dear Henry.

With water, dear Henry, dear Henry, with water!

9

With what shall I fetch it, dear Liza, dear Liza?

With what shall I fetch it, dear Liza, with what?

With a bucket, dear Henry, dear Henry, dear Henry.

With a bucket, dear Henry, dear Henry, a bucket!

10

There's a hole in the bucket, dear Liza, dear Liza.

There's a hole in the bucket, dear Liza, a hole.

Five lit-tle ducks went swim-ming one day, o-ver the pond and far a-way.

Ma-ma Duck said, "Quack quack quack quack," and on-ly four lit-tle ducks came back.

Four lit-tle ducks went swim-ming one day, o-ver the pond and far a-way.

Ma-ma Duck said, "Quack quack quack quack," and on-ly three lit-tle ducks came back.

Three lit-tle ducks went swim-ming one day, o-ver the pond and far a-way.

Ma-ma Duck said, "Quack quack quack quack," and on-ly two lit-tle ducks came back.

Two lit-tle ducks went swim-ming one day, o-ver the pond and far a-way.

Ma-ma Duck said, "Quack quack quack quack," and on-ly one lit-tle duck came back.

One lit-tle duck went swim-ming one day, o-ver the pond and far a-way.

Ma-ma Duck said, "Quack quack quack quack," and no lit-tle duck came swim-ming back.

Ma—ma Duck went swim-ming one day, o-ver the pond and far a-way.

Ma-ma Duck said, "Quack quack quack quack," and five lit-tle ba-by ducks came swim-ming back.

11

A-tisket,

A-tis-ket, a-tas-ket
A green and yel-low bas-ket.
I wrote a let-ter to my love
And on the way I dropped it.
I dropped it
I dropped it

12

A-tasket

6 And on the way I dropped it.

7 A lit-tle boy picked it up

8 And put it in his pock-et!

13

Tin-ga-lay—o! Run, lit-tle don-key, run!

My don-key eats

hiccup

My don-key sleeps

My don-key kicks with his two hind feet.

Tin-ga-lay—o! Run, lit-tle don-key, run! Tin-ga-lay—o! Run, lit-tle don-key, run!

This old man, he played three.

He played knick-knack on my knee. (refrain)

This old man, he played four.

He played knick-knack on my door. (refrain)

OLD MAN

this old man came rol-ling home!

This old man, he played five.

He played knick-knack on my hive. (refrain)

This old man, he played se-ven.

He played knick-knack up to Hea-ven. (refrain)

This old man, he played six.

He played knick-knack with some sticks. (refrain)

If you're hap-py and you know it, clap your hands! (clap!) (clap!)

If you're hap-py and you know it, clap your hands! (clap!) (clap!)

If you're hap-py and you know it, and you real-ly want to show it

If you're hap-py and you know it, clap your hands! (clap!) (clap!)

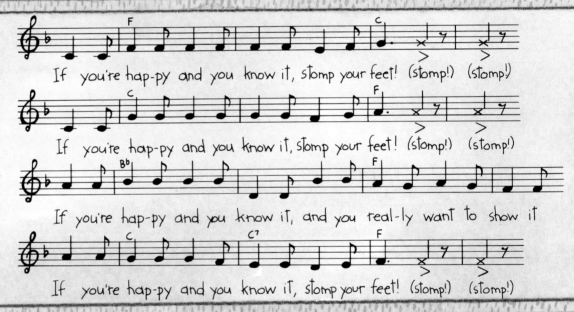

If you're hap-py and you know it, stomp your feet! (stomp!) (stomp!)

If you're hap-py and you know it, stomp your feet! (stomp!) (stomp!)

If you're hap-py and you know it, and you real-ly want to show it

If you're hap-py and you know it, stomp your feet! (stomp!) (stomp!)

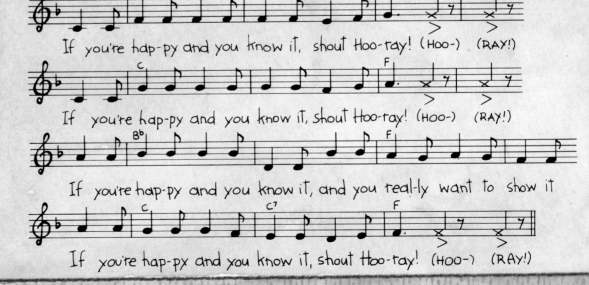

If you're hap-py and you know it, shout Hoo-ray! (Hoo-) (RAY!)

If you're hap-py and you know it, shout Hoo-ray! (Hoo-) (RAY!)

If you're hap-py and you know it, and you real-ly want to show it

If you're hap-py and you know it, shout Hoo-ray! (HOO-) (RAY!)

and YOU KNOW IT

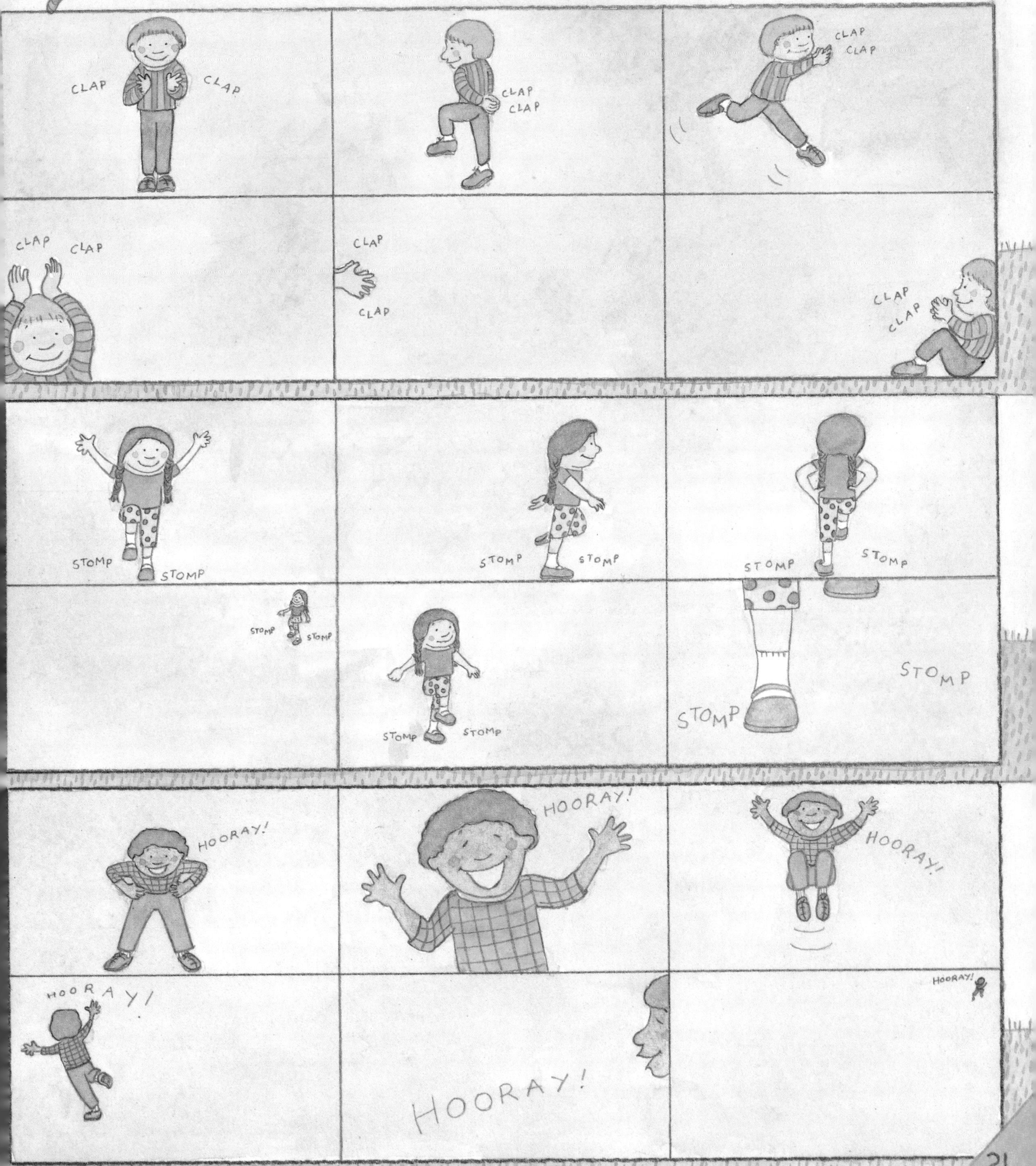

The bear went o-ver the moun-tain, the bear went o-ver the moun-tain, the bear went o-ver the moun-tain,

To see what he could see—! To see what he could see—! To see what he could see—!

The o-ther side of the moun-tain, the o-ther side of the moun-tain,

the o-ther side of the moun-tain, was all that he could see —!

23

Comin' Through

If a bo-dy meet a bo-dy com-in' through the rye—

If a bo-dy kiss a bo-dy, need a bo-dy cry?

the Rye

Ev-ery las-sie has her lad-die; None, they say, have I, yet

All the lads they smile on me, when com-in' through the rye.

25

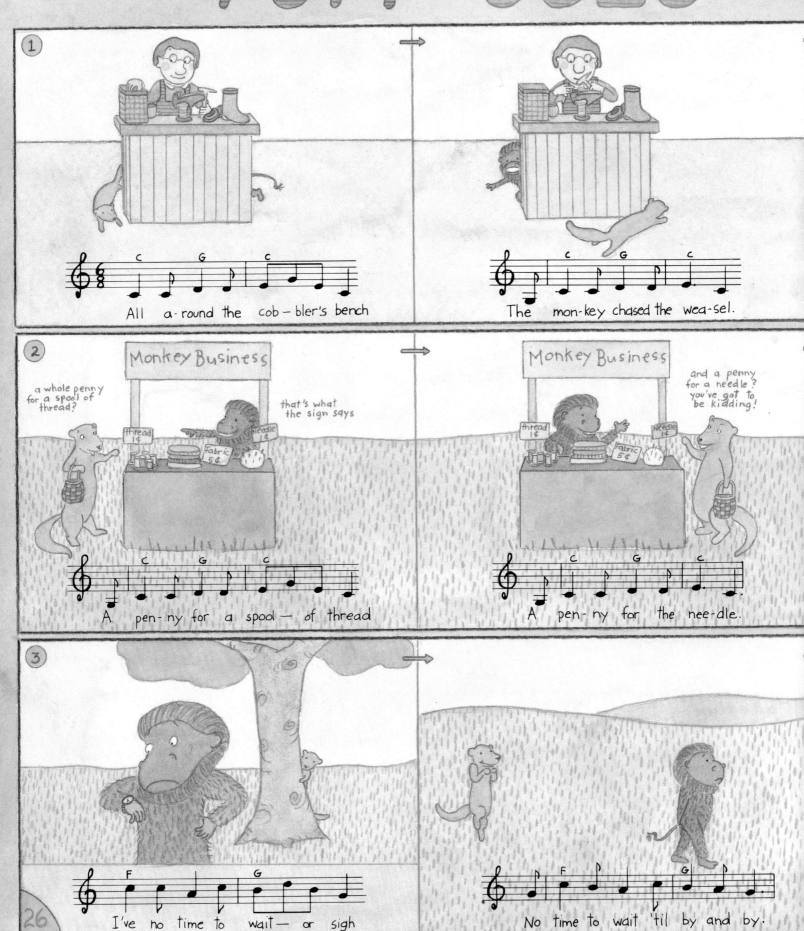

THE WEASEL

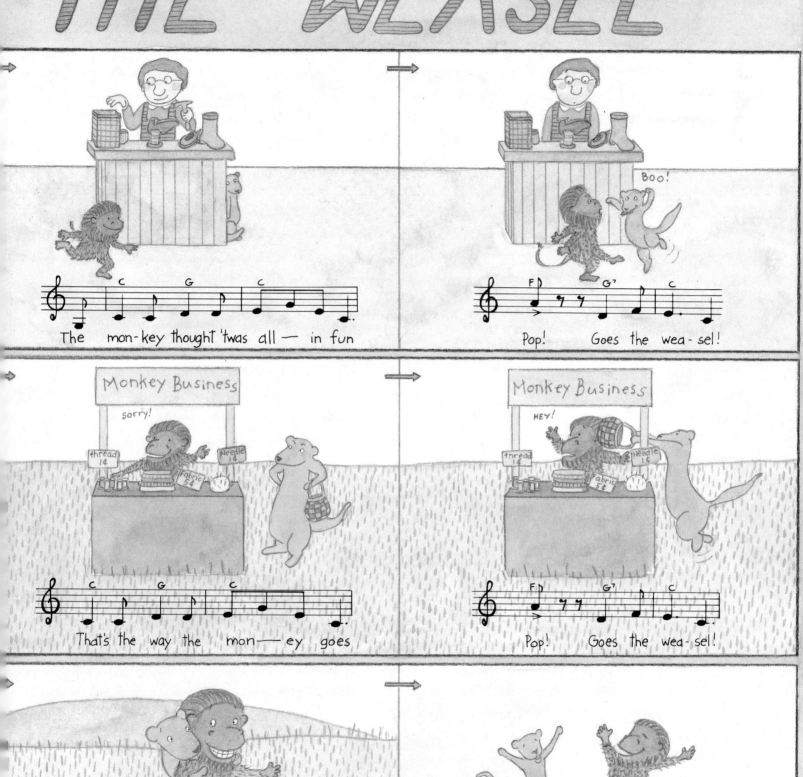

SILK HAT

Chris-to-pher Co-lum-bus, now what do you think of that?   A big, fat la-dy sat u-pon my hat!

My hat she broke and that's no joke, my hat she broke and that's no joke!

Chris-to-pher Co-lum-bus, now what do you think of that?

Kook-a-bur-ra sits in the old gum tree—

Mer-ry mer-ry king of the bush is he—

Laugh, Kook-a-bur-ra

Laugh, Kook-a-bur-ra

Gay your life must be!

Kookaburra

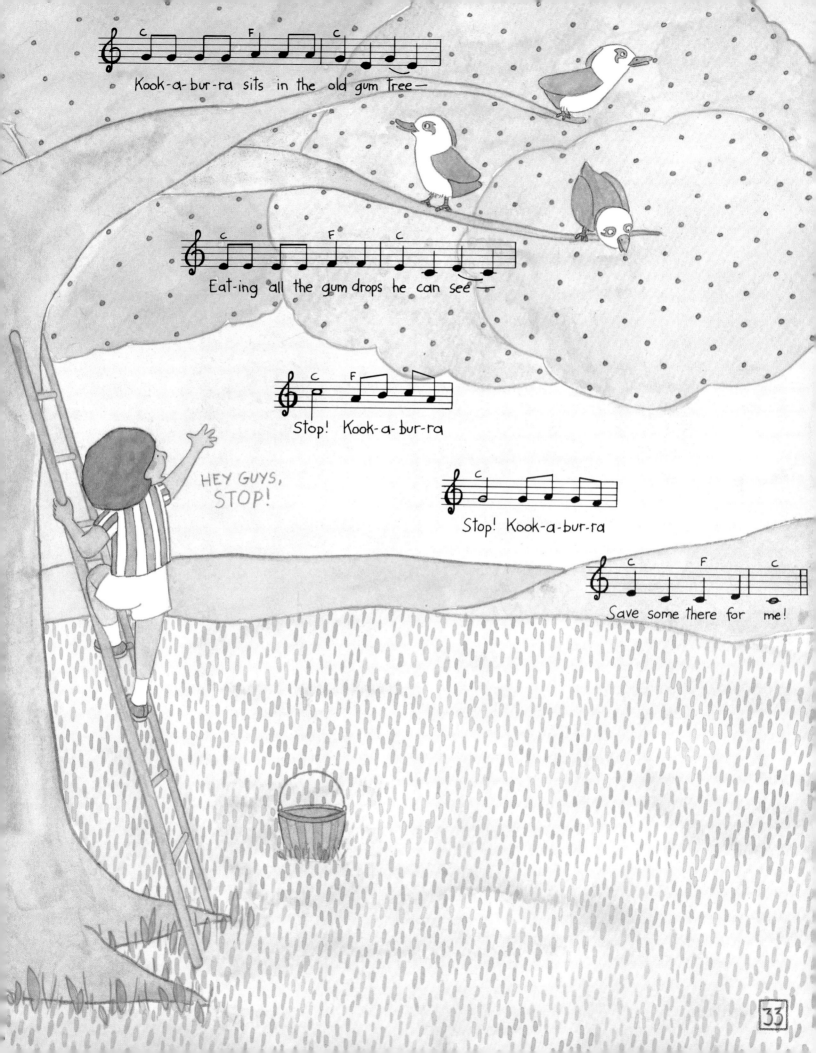

Kook-a-bur-ra sits in the old gum tree—

Eat-ing all the gum drops he can see—

Stop! Kook-a-bur-ra

Stop! Kook-a-bur-ra

Save some there for me!

HEY GUYS, STOP!

★ ROLL OVER ★

There were ten in the bed and the lit-tle one said,

"Roll o-ver! Roll o-ver!"

So they all rolled o-ver and one fell out. There were nine

in the bed and the lit-tle one said, "Roll o-ver! Roll o-ver!"

So they all rolled o-ver and one fell out. There were eight

in the bed and the lit-tle one said, "Roll o-ver! Roll o-ver!"

So they all rolled o-ver and one fell out. There were sev-en

in the bed and the lit-tle one said, "Roll o-ver! Roll o-ver!"

So they all rolled o-ver and one fell out. There were six

in the bed and the lit-tle one said, "Roll o-ver! Roll o-ver!"

34

★ ROLL OVER ★

So they all rolled o-ver and one fell out. There were five

in the bed and the lit-tle one said, "Roll o-ver! Roll o-ver!"

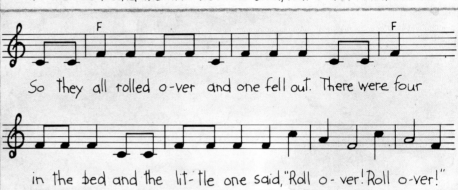

So they all rolled o-ver and one fell out. There were four

in the bed and the lit-tle one said, "Roll o-ver! Roll o-ver!"

So they all rolled o-ver and one fell out. There were three

in the bed and the lit-tle one said, "Roll o-ver! Roll o-ver!"

So they all rolled o-ver and one fell out. There were two

in the bed and the lit-tle one said, "Roll o-ver! Roll o-ver!"

So they all rolled o-ver and one fell out. There was one

in the bed and that lit-tle one said, "Good night!"

LITTLE DOG GONE?

With his tail cut short and his ears cut long

Oh where, oh where can he be ———?

And if the tail were more strong than he

Why the tail would wag-gle the dog ———!

NOTES ON THE SONGS

"In a Cabin" is a traditional song that is often sung with accompanying hand motions.

"Do Your Ears Hang Low?" comes from the American Revolutionary War period, and is often sung with accompanying hand motions.

"There's a Hole in the Bucket" is Pennsylvania Dutch in origin.

"Five Little Ducks" is an American counting song that is often sung with accompanying hand motions.

"A-tisket, A-tasket" is a traditional Anglo–American song.

"Tingalayo" comes from the island of Martinique in the West Indies, and is often sung with accompanying hand motions.

"This Old Man" is a traditional counting-game song from England.

"The Animal Fair" is a nineteenth century minstrel song. The song is often left open-ended, concluding with a repetition of the lyric, "the monk, the monk, the monk . . ."

"If You're Happy and You Know It" is probably an American song. Additional verses can be added by inventing new endings to the lyric, "If you're happy and you know it . . ."

"The Bear Went Over the Mountain"'s melody comes from a French song, *"Malbrouck S'en Va-t-en Guerre."* With different words it became a traditional American song.

"Comin' Through the Rye" is from Scotland.

"Pop! Goes the Weasel" is a traditional song from seventeenth century England. It made its way to America with the Pilgrims. Many versions of the song are to be found. It is believed to reflect hard times, when people had to "pop" (pawn) their "weasels" (tools of their trade, such as leather, nails, and hammers for a cobbler).

"My Tall Silk Hat"'s melody comes from *"Funiculi Funicula,"* by L. Denza, who wrote it in 1880 to honor the opening of the funicular railway that went to the top of Mt. Vesuvius.

"Oh Dear, What Can the Matter Be?" is from late eighteenth century England, and made its way to America after the American Revolution.

"Kookaburra" is from Australia, and may be sung as a round. A kookaburra is a bird about the size of a crow, and its call can sound like laughter.

"Roll Over, Roll Over" is an American folk song.

"Where Has My Little Dog Gone?" was originally a German folk tune. In 1864 American composer Septimus Winner wrote the first verse; the second verse was added to make a college song in the late 1800's.

"Hush, Little Baby" was originally from England. It made its way to the Appalachian Mountain region, and then spread throughout America.

SOURCES FOR THE NOTES:
Folk Songs of Many Lands, by Grace Castagnetta (New York: Simon and Schuster), 1938. The Great Rounds Songbook, by Esther L. Nelson (New York: Sterling Publishing Co.), 1985. Lullabies from Around the World, by Lynne Knudsen (New York: A Rutledge Book/Follett Publication Co.), 1967. More Songs to Grow On, by Beatrice Landeck (New York: William Morrow & Co.), 1954. The Reader's Digest Children's Songbook, William L. Simon, ed. (Pleasantville, N.Y.: Reader's Digest Association), 1985. The Songs We Sang, by Theodore Raph (New York: A. S. Barnes & Co.), 1964. Tom Glazer's Treasury of Songs for Children, compiled by Tom Glazer (Scarborough, N.Y.: Songs Music), 1964.